School Milk

Claudia Court

Published by Dempsey & Windle

15 Rosetrees
Guildford
Surrey
GU1 2HS
UK
01483 571164
dempseyandwindle.com
A catalogue record for this book is available from the British Library

British Library Cataloguing-in-Publication Data

ISBN: 978-1-913329-72-3

Printed and bound in the UK

For Gillian
who was there through the pint-sized years
and saw it all

Acknowledgements

I am hugely grateful to the poet Colin Pink, who recently invented the triadic couplet form which I have used throughout this book.

Thanks also to fellow poets at the Barnes and Chiswick Stanza, and at Lisa Kelly's Torriano workshop, for their support and feedback.

Contents

Pint-sized

8   Viewpoint
9   Why Didn't She Say So?
10 Multi-tasking
11 School Milk
12 Tuck Shop
13 Sister Act
14 Sports Day
15 Reverend Mother
16 First Communion
17 Eleven Plus

Full cream

19 Boarding
20 Grotto
21 Fire Practice
22 Uniform
23 Old Habits
24 Pockets
25 Hard-wired
26 Homage-on-the-run
27 Playing Our Cards Right
28 Folk Mass
29 Pressing Business
30 The Body and Blood
31 Veiled Threat
32 Chapel

Pint-sized

Viewpoint

It's playtime and Danny is standing by
the swings, trying to look up our skirts.

As we go higher, I can see over the wall
into the vegetable patch, where Sister Ann

is talking to Father Bob. They are leaning
against the greenhouse. And each other.

Why Didn't She Say So?

My first full day at school, aged four
and it's going well. I've eaten lunch

sung a song, found a friend. But now
Sister Ann says we're to make a basket.

I can't…I don't know how…my chair's wet!
Turns out, she wants me to fold my hands.

Multi-tasking

Sister Attracta sweeps up her skirts
and tucks them out of harm's way.

She is still gripping a piece of chalk
from class, in her teeth. She swings

her axe easily, the pile of logs grows.
She sings to the Lord, wrings a hen's neck.

School Milk

Squat, third-pint bottles have been thawing
near the radiator. Chunks of ice remain.

We watch Sister's breath as she speaks,
suck through straws, shiver with delight

then freeze as Danny starts to slurp out loud
goes too far, gets the cane.

Tuck Shop

Sherbet dabs, flying saucers, gob
stoppers, candy shrimps, aniseed

balls: we clamour round the small
table while Sister Martha snatches

our coins in her ample fist,
chewing vigorously as she works.

Sister Act

May we treat each other kindly,
she intones, *be gentle as lambs.*

Poor Danny gets the giggles and
quick as a flash, she's at his side

ruler raised, sharp edge slicing down
on upturned knuckles, drawing blood.

Sports Day

Like a sergeant she drills us: we run
there and back, stumble in sacks

hop with three legs, carry eggs
on a spoon, win nervous applause.

Even the parents take part, leaping
to attention at Sister's fierce whistle.

Reverend Mother

Reverend Mother enjoys felling trees.
She's been hacking away at a birch

in front of us all playtime and when
its tall trunk creaks, she shrieks

Stand back! and everyone flees – except
for her. She lies, felled by her tree.

First Communion

We line up to kneel at the altar –
eight small brides with lace veils

eight small boys with white shorts.
Even Danny is standing tall.

Our first wafer, that sip of wine:
nothing can stop us now.

Eleven Plus

Frilly twists of wood-shaving tumble
onto desks as we grind in silence.

Our pencils sharpened, Sister makes
the sign of the cross, says we may begin.

I jab the page with my thoughts, while
Danny stabs his leg through his shorts.

Full cream

Boarding

I spend my first night in terror
as I listen to the huge monster

growling and prowling outside
our dormitory. I am still shaking

at breakfast, when they ask:
Did you hear Matron, snoring?

Grotto

We are gathered around the grotto
in scratchy Sunday best. Bees hum

rosaries hang, Sister Clare begins:
May our prayers be whispers like

angels' wings… Father Tom's motorbike
roars up the drive. *Ahh, men*, she sighs.

Fire Practice

We stumble into the night, yawning
and shivering in pyjamas – it's four a.m.

and the shrillness of the fire bell fills
our ears. *At least we'll see what nuns*

wear to bed, hisses Jo. But they are all
fully dressed; perhaps they never sleep.

Uniform

Two pairs of brown lace-ups (one for
Sundays), gym shoes, ballet pumps

Wellingtons, outdoor plimsolls, hockey
boots and slippers: our feet have it good.

Less so our pride, as we sweep past
in crimson cloaks and the skinheads jeer.

Old Habits

Every nun wears a wimple, protruding
to shield the sides of her face.

We do as we please, they seldom see –
then *Vatican II* says wimples can go.

We wave goodbye to our freedom
while the Sisters rejoice at theirs.

Pockets

Jo stuffs hers with unwanted fried
bread from breakfast, grease seeping

through flannel skirt. Mine are for letters,
savoured in the quiet of class. The nuns

use theirs for greying handkerchiefs;
rosaries; and confiscated letters.

Hard-wired

We'd wake to a holy water dispenser
thrust at our side in murmured prayer:

we'd make the sign of the cross
with hand still limp from sleep. Such

was the ritual, I still catch my whispered
Amen in the dim of an autumn dawn.

Homage-on-the-run

Skidding to a halt along the polished
corridor, I curtsy briefly to Our Lady's

portrait. We are required to do this
each time we pass Reverend Mother too –

there have been several twisted ankles.
Matron says nuns are not royalty.

Playing Our Cards Right

An occasional flush of the loo seems
to keep Sister Clare at bay. We squat

in the harsh strip light, playing whist
and gin rummy – too bored to sleep.

Then, at judicious intervals, we creep
back to bed. It's always a gamble.

Folk Mass

We wrestle our guitars into position
in the narrow pew and begin to strum

Kumbaya. Only three voices
have joined in. Sister starts to clap.

Father Tom rolls his eyes, reaches
for the cup of communion wine.

Pressing Business

To assuage midnight hunger, we sneak
to the laundry room and iron ourselves

some toast. We iron our hair too
to make it straight. Tonight, Irma's curls

simply bubble and sizzle and stick –
someone has tried to make Welsh rarebit.

The Body and Blood

A tacit excusal from Games,
aspirin quietly proffered –

womanhood is something
even nuns can't control

while we, on the brink of all
we hope to be, grow pale.

Veiled Threat

She was always furious, face puce
with pent-up rage as she hurled books

across the classroom at our heads.
Her husband and son were both killed

in a car crash. She became a nun
to escape the pain. Or redirect it.

Chapel

There's something about falling
to your knees in a place layered

with incense, whispered prayer
the fading notes of an organ:

you feel revived, uplifted, pure.
You almost see how nuns happen.

*How to Punctuate a Silence (***2020)**

If you have enjoyed *School Milk*, you may also like Claudia
Court's debut collection.

"Claudia Court is a striking new voice – lyrical, spare,
mysterious, presenting richly-crafted poems informed by
clarity and feeling."

Katherine Gallagher

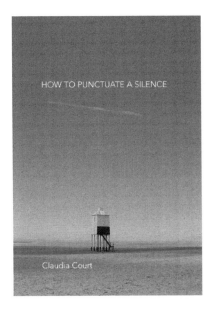

Reviews of *How to Punctuate a Silence*

"Claudia Court has a real talent for representing the way people speak, but also, choose not to speak, to each other, as well as themselves. The silences of this book are compelling, original, eloquent, and always audible."

Sam Smith, *The Journal*

"Claudia Court addresses the subjects of love, loss and illness with sensitivity and wit. Her empathy is apparent in poems about others' problems and in tender portraits of her family that don't gloss over difficulties. Whether in free verse, syllabics, haiku or rhyme, her poetry impresses with its honesty, clarity and economy; 'words recognise my hurt, they soothe me', she writes, and her words do the same for us."

Stephen Claughton

"How can words clothe the abyss of silence and comfort us in times of need? In her poetry Court uses words, by turns witty and poignant, that weave together the experience of love and loss, pain and pleasure, ordinary and extraordinary moments. Often in life, as Eliot says, we have the experience but miss the meaning; holding onto a strong cord of hope Court's poems help us find our way through the labyrinth of life.'

Colin Pink

These are unrushed poems that demand our attention through their quality of address, their clear-eyed look at life and for the silences that are as alive and as varied as the words which precede and follow in an intricate and absorbing dance.'

Lisa Kelly